Indoor Playground Vision

A Guide to Launching a Fun-Filled Children's Center

Table of Contents

Chapter 1. Introduction

Whether you're an aspiring entrepreneur with a heart for children's joy or an established business owner looking to diversify your venture, join us as we dive into a wonderful, fun-filled world of opportunities in the industry of indoor play areas. This special report, titled "Indoor Playground Vision: A Guide to Launching a Fun-Filled Children's Center," paints a vivid picture of the captivating joy, limitless creativity, and transformative ROI a colorful, buzzing children's center can offer. Filled with actionable insights, practical how-tos, expert opinions, and success stories, this report is your comprehensive guide on how to bring life to your indoor playground vision. Unwrap the potential of this brilliant business idea, one playful idea at a time! Let the laughter begin.

Chapter 2. Setting the Stage: A Snippet of the Children's Recreational Industry

Recreation for children has been a growing market for several years. The increasing complexity of the modern world, the rise of dual-income families, and the evolution of teaching and learning practices have all created a perfect storm for the development and proliferation of children's recreational centers.

2.1. The Historical Perspective

The notion of recreation for children has changed drastically over the years. Traditional forms of play included outdoor activities, board games, and imaginative play, like setting up dollhouses or playing pretend school.

The advent of technology slowly ushered in a new era of recreational activities. Video games began occupying the leisure hours of children worldwide, marking the first significant shift. This transition, however, also brought with it a range of health issues, including sedentary lifestyles leading to childhood obesity, eyesight challenges, and decreased social skills.

The subsequent realization of these health impacts started a movement back towards physical play, albeit with the comfort and safety of being indoors. Indoor recreational centers, combining the best of traditional play and technological advancements, began cropping up worldwide.

2.2. Evolving Market Dynamics

Now, the children's recreational industry is a thriving segment of the larger recreational market. According to estimates from IBISWorld, the indoor play centers' market size in the U.S alone was $3 billion in 2020 and projected to grow further. Globally, the prospects look even better with a Compound Annual Growth Rate (CAGR) of 10.2%, expected over the next six years as per Grand View Research reports.

One should note that the aforementioned statistics, impressive as they are, came despite the COVID-19 pandemic's dampening effects. The bounce back in post-pandemic times makes the sector one of the most promising ones for anyone contemplating entering this industry.

2.3. Anatomy of a Successful Indoor Playground

A successful indoor playground constitutes several key factors. First of these is a safe environment. The play equipment, flooring, food preparation areas, hygiene practices, and staff training all need to ensure the utmost safety.

Secondly, companies must incorporate a variety of play options to cater to different age groups and promote skill development – from facilities for physical activities, like a ball pit or climbing frames, to creative spaces, for arts, crafts, or role-play games, and zones for relaxation.

Lastly, the successful incorporation of technology, like virtual reality or augmented reality games, can provide an edge over competitors and make the playground stand out.

2.4. The Role of Design in Play Centers

The design of an indoor playground can significantly impact its success. The selection of play equipment, their positioning, color schemes, and overall ambiance all capture children's imagination and parents' trust. Essentially, the aim should be to create a space that is as entertaining for children as it is relaxing and reassuring for the parents who accompany them.

In the never-ending pursuit of dazzle and delightful experiences, the aesthetics of a children's recreational center can ignite a child's creativity, encouraging them to explore, learn, and make memories, all while ensuring their safety and comfort.

2.5. Regulatory Environment

Ensuring safety in your indoor playground also ties in directly with complying with international safety standards and local regulations. Requirements may vary by country, but they generally encompass fire safety, food safety, equipment safety, and hygiene standards. Regular inspections and certifications by recognized bodies can enhance a center's credibility and ensure strict adherence to safety norms.

Additionally, ensuring inclusive design can significantly add value and attract a wider audience. Play areas should be accessible to children of various abilities and cater to special needs, wherever possible.

2.6. The Business Model and Revenue Streams

An indoor playground can generate revenue through various models. The most straightforward being the entry fee, which can be a flat-rate or time-based. Supplementary streams include income from food and beverage sales, merchandise, party bookings, workshops, and events.

A subscription or membership model, providing benefits like regular discounts, freebies, and priority access to events, can further augment revenues and ensure customer loyalty.

2.7. To Conclude

The children's indoor play area industry is an exciting, dynamic, and potentially rewarding business opportunity. It contributes positively to the overall development of a child, providing a safe, enjoyable, and stimulating environment. This guide presents a detailed insight into the industry and the various elements it encompasses. The further chapters will dive deeper into each of these topics, providing actionable strategies and tips to make your vision of launching a fun-filled children's center a reality.

Chapter 3. Building Blocks: Crafting Your Unique Indoor Playground Vision

Each successful journey starts with a vision, and the same rings true when planning to build an indoor playground. The vision sets the course and creates a foundation upon which all decisions are built. It holds the identity of your venture and stipulates what you strive for. Hence, crafting your unique vision will be the stepping stone to your triumphant path in the industry of indoor play areas.

3.1. Identifying Your Core Values

Selecting your core values is a crucial initial step as it firmly roots your venture, shaping its character, culture, and decisions. These values become the guiding principles that dictate your business. For instance, principles might be rooted in providing an entertaining, educational, and safe environment for children.

When you identify your core values, consider the following questions: what are the values that you and your team hold dear? What values do you wish to impart to your customers? What standards will you commit to uphold no matter what happens? Answers to these questions will help you solidify your core values.

3.2. Creating a Vision Statement

The vision statement is a future-oriented declaration of your business's purpose and aspirations. It conveys both the purpose and values of your company. In crafting a vision statement, aim to incorporate the high-level goals that are most important to you. The vision statement should ideally inspire and motivate you and your team, all the while giving direction to guide decision-making on a day-to-day basis.

Typically, a great vision statement should be short and simple, but nonetheless potent and inspiring. And remember, your vision statement isn't what you 'do', it's what you 'strive for'. For instance, an indoor playground's vision statement might be "To foster creativity, fun, and learning in a safe and well-supervised environment".

3.3. Defining Your Mission Statement

Unlike the vision statement, which is forward-looking, the mission statement focuses on today and what your business does. While your vision statement might remain unchanged for ten or even twenty years, your mission statement should be updated as needed to reflect the dynamic nature of your business.

The mission statement includes the practical ways you will execute your vision. It outlines the key reasons why your business exists, why it's valuable, and how it aims to serve its customers—the children and parents. It should answer questions such as: What do we do? How do we do it? Who do we do it for? What value do we bring?

For an indoor playground, an example could be "To provide an inclusive, fun-filled and stimulating environment for children where they can play, learn, and grow, in concert with ensuring comfort and relaxation for parents."

3.4. Analyzing Your Target Market

Understanding your customer base is quintessential in defining your indoor playground vision. This includes understanding the children's preferences as well as the parent's expectations. Using surveys, focus groups, and market research can deliver insights on this matter.

Consider your target market's demographics and psychographics. Demographics will cover physical factors like age, gender, and location, while psychographics will deal with psychological factors like preferences, behavior, and expectations.

3.5. Scoping Out the Competition

Knowing your competition is vital in shaping a unique business proposition. To differentiate your playground from the rest, you need to do something different, something better, something memorable.

By assessing your competition, identify what they do well and where they fall short. It doesn't necessarily mean copying what works well for them but rather learning from their successes and mistakes.

3.6. Crafting the Unique Value Proposition

After analyzing your target market and competition, now comes the process of crafting your unique value proposition, or UVP. Your UVP is an avenue for you to put forth your unique strengths and demonstrate why customers should choose your indoor playground over others.

It's crucial that your UVP addresses a specific customer need or demand and resonates well with your target audience. It could be a unique play concept never seen before, an impeccable safety record, educational play options, comfort and convenience features for parents, or special services for birthday parties and events.

3.7. Bringing It All Together

Having defined all the foundations of your vision, now is the time to bring it all together. What you have is a vision that reflects your core values, a potent vision statement that serves as your north star, a dynamic mission statement that outlines your day-to-day operations, a good grasp of your target market, an insight into your competition, and a compelling unique value proposition.

With all of these in place, you will not only have a unique vision for your indoor playground but a strategic roadmap to your destination. Remember that fulfilling your vision and mission is an ongoing process, continually evaluate your progress, take note of critical lessons, and be prepared to refine your plans as necessary. You are now ready to step into the fascinating and rewarding world of indoor playgrounds!

Chapter 4. More than Fun and Games: Why Indoor Playgrounds Matter

Indoor playgrounds are more than just places of leisure where kids run around, slide, and climb to their heart's content. At the core, they are fertile grounds for learning and development, presenting an opportunity for children to explore, interact, and push their boundaries in a safe and controlled environment.

4.1. The Significance of Play

Play is not an optional or frivolous activity for children. Rather, it is recognized as an integral aspect of childhood by the United Nations High Commission for Human Rights due to its critical role in a child's cognitive, physical, social, and emotional well-being.

In 2007, the American Academy of Pediatrics (AAP) released a pivotal clinical report titled 'The Importance of Play in Promoting Healthy Child Development and Maintaining Strong Parent-Child Bonds.' AAP highlighted play as being vital for children to develop creativity, dexterity, physical, cognitive, and emotional strength. It specifically pointed out that it through play children at a very early age engage and interact in the world around them.

Moreover, studies have shown that play at an early age can help prepare a child's developing brain for life by stimulating the formation of connections between the brain's billions of nerve cells. Play also allows children to create and explore a world they can control while conquering their fears and practicing adult roles, sometimes in conjunction with other children or adult caregivers.

4.2. Good for Children, Good for Parents

Indoor playgrounds offer a safe, supervised space for children to play regardless of weather conditions. These environments allow children to interact with their peers, engaging their social and emotional capabilities and developing real-life skills such as sharing, negotiation, and leadership.

Parents, on the other hand, benefit from the peace of mind that comes with knowing their children are safe in a controlled environment. Indoor play centers also offer an opportunity for parents to connect, build a network, and find support amongst each other while their kids play. Furthermore, parents can also see first-hand how their children are interacting with others, recognize their strengths and areas that need development, and engage directly in their child's play. This interaction supports the formation of strong parent-child bonds.

Indoor playgrounds also open opportunities for families to spend quality time together. Unlike outdoor playgrounds, indoor facilities cater to a more extensive range of activities suitable for both children and adults, making it a fun family outing option.

4.3. The Educational Aspect of Indoor Play Centres

The incorporation of educational elements in playground equipment is a significant opportunity that indoor playgrounds present. While children are drawn to these centers purely for entertainment and pleasure, incorporating learning elements in equipment brings a great value addition.

Role-play areas, climbing frames, soft play equipment, sensory items, tactile boards, and interactive panels cater to children's varying developmental stages whilst keeping them engaged and entertained. It creates a learning-through-play environment, a balance between education and entertainment.

This inclusion of educational toys and activities can also involve parents and caregivers to encourage developmental growth further. By offering activities that can be performed in teams or with an adult, indoor playgrounds can foster their social-emotional development and create a nurturing environment for their intellectual growth.

4.4. Health Benefits of Physical Activity in Playgrounds

Where indoor playgrounds truly shine is in their promotion of physical health. According to the World Health Organization, childhood obesity is one of the most serious public health challenges of the 21st century. Regular physical activity can help prevent numerous health issues like obesity, heart disease, diabetes, and even mental health disorders in children.

Indoor playgrounds' structures are designed for children to climb, hang, jump, run, slide, all which require and promote physical activities. They also encourage children to challenge themselves physically, promote motor skill development, spatial and directional awareness, hand-to-eye coordination, agility, and flexibility.

4.5. The Psychological Impact of Indoor Playgrounds

Apart from the physical benefits, indoor playgrounds can also contribute to the healthy psychological development of children. The fun and stimulating environment of these playgrounds can enhance a child's ability to focus, stimulating their mind and improving their concentration.

In conclusion, indoor playgrounds are much more than fun and games; they play an irreplaceable role in a child's overall development – physically, mentally, and socially. They represent a unique tool that can significantly contribute towards making childhood a joyful, educational, and healthy journey, all under a safe and controlled environment. As they continue to evolve with the incorporation of technology and creative play options, the benefits they offer children only stand to increase.

For entrepreneurs, they represent an opportunity to tap into an industry that is not just about profits, but about contributing positively to society. Ultimately, the success of an indoor playground business is not just measured by its ROI but by the smiles and laughter they bring, and the difference they make in children's lives, one playful day at a time.

Chapter 5. The Blueprint: Designing a Safe and Stimulating Environment

Safety standards are not only a key component of any indoor playground design, but they are also legally mandatory. A safe environment is paramount for parents' peace of mind and is a crucial consideration when children are involved. While safety is a top priority, the design of your playground should also inspire fun and stimulate children's creative minds.

5.1. Understanding Child Development

Child development is a continuous process that revolves around various parameters such as cognitive, physical, social, and emotional growth. Thus, understanding the intricacies of child development can aid in the design of a playground that suits various age groups, developmental stages, and abilities.

In designing a playground, consider the ages of the children who will be using the facility. Children's skills and interests change as they develop, so the playground should reflect this progression. For example, infant areas should have softer, smoother surfaces where they can safely crawl. Toddlers, on the other hand, are much more active, thus requiring physical activities like a mini slide or soft play blocks. For older kids, integrate more challenging structures since they will enjoy testing their limits.

5.2. Catering to Diverse Abilities

Inclusivity should be ingrained in every design aspect of your indoor playground. Create an environment that is welcoming and accommodating for all kids, including ones with disabilities. Installing ramps for wheelchair users, providing sensory games for children with autism, and ensuring clear signage for visually impaired kids are just a few measures that can make the playground a space for all.

5.3. Safety Features and Maintenance

In terms of safety, every design aspect matters, from the selection of non-toxic materials, ensuring correct installation, to the maintenance of equipment. Prevention is fundamental in accident management. Considering the safety features during the design phase can substantially reduce the risk of injuries. Some safety features include padding the floors and walls, creating barriers around the playground, and making all play equipment sturdy and secure.

Regular maintenance is essential to extend the longevity of your playground and ensure that it remains safe. Make sure that weakened structures are repaired immediately, worn-out parts are replaced timely, and the entire facility is kept clean.

5.4. Choosing the Right Equipment

While choosing equipment for your indoor playground, consider equipment that provides a balance between providing physical activity and cultivating creativity. This can include things like slides, obstacle courses, reading corners, and imaginative play stations. Make sure to include both physically energetic activities and quiet areas for reading or other calming activities within your design.

5.5. Creating a Stimulating Environment

The aesthetics of your indoor playground present a wonderful opportunity to stimulate children's senses and spark their imaginations. Incorporating vibrant colors, murals, and textured surfaces can make the playground visually appealing, while tactile elements can help promote fine motor skills.

Don't shy away from incorporating technology, as long as it's interactive and educational. For example, touch screens with puzzle-solving games, or projectors that create interactive floors can serve as mental stimuli for kids.

5.6. Zoning Your Playground

Logical zoning is crucial in managing space effectively and maintaining the flow of activities on the playground. A well-zoned playground allows segregation of different activities, determines the movement pattern of the children, and helps in crowd control.

Zones should be made according to the age groups and activities, and two distinctly different zones should not overlap. For example, have separate areas for the toddler zone, active play zone, calming corner, and creative zone.

In conclusion, the layout and design of your indoor playground significantly define the kind of experience you offer to the children and their caregivers. Attention to safety, understanding the fundamentals of child development, considering inclusivity, careful selection of equipment, creating a stimulating environment, and efficient zoning can all contribute to a safe and engaging indoor playground. Your aim should be to strike a balance between safety and fun, while constantly striving to provide a platform that nurtures the all-round development of a child.

Design with passion, design with care, and let the child's laughter be your greatest reward.

Chapter 6. Licensed to Thrill: Navigating Legalities and Permissions

Starting a business that is meant to bring so much joy to others has its own peculiar challenges, just like any other entrepreneurial venture. Yet one area many burgeoning entrepreneurs struggle with is understanding the legalities and permissions required to launch an indoor playground. The administrative task of building a children's play center goes beyond leasing a space and buying play equipment. Before you welcome your first batch of giggling visitors, you must ensure your enterprise is legally sound and has all the required permits.

6.1. Navigating the Maze: Understanding Laws and Regulations

Laws and regulations on children's play areas vary greatly from country to country, and even from city to city within the same nation. Therefore, it is essential to familiarize yourself with local, state, and federal laws governing the operation of indoor play spaces. Usually, these laws touch on aspects such as safety regulations, hygiene standards, zoning laws, and business registration rules.

Firstly, you should begin by conducting extensive online research or seeking consultation from a business lawyer who is well-versed with such laws. Remember, breaches of these laws can lead to hefty fines or, worse, legal litigations that might prematurely close your doors.

6.2. Checkmate: Dealing with Zoning Laws

Zoning laws impact where you can set up your indoor playground business. These are laws that divide a town, city, or the county into zones, with specific specifications for each zone.

You need to identify whether your proposed location falls under commercial, residential, industrial, or mixed-use zoning. Since the indoor playground is a commercial venture, you need to find a location that falls under commercial or mixed-use zoning.

6.3. Child's Play: Securing Business Registration and Licenses

To legally operate your business, you need to be registered. Depending on your jurisdiction and what type of business entity (be it a sole proprietorship, partnership, or corporation) you're planning on, various forms and fees will be required.

Once the business entity registration is complete, there are still more licenses to secure. At a minimum, you'll need an operating license or permit from your city or county. In some cases, you are also required to obtain special licenses pertaining to child care or entertainment services. Don't forget to carry out regular renewal of these licenses based on the stipulated timelines.

6.4. Safety First: Ensuring your Play Equipment Meets Standards

Safety regulations for indoor playgrounds primarily cover the play equipment and general playground design. The laws usually dictate everything from the type of material used in play equipment to the playground's design, aimed at reducing injuries.

In the United States, for instance, there are ASTM International standards and guidelines you must adhere to when setting up the playground equipment. There's a European equivalent under EN standards. Your playground equipment supplier should provide you with a certificate ensuring the products meet the required standards.

Moreover, you should routinely carry out maintenance and safety checks on your equipment to ensure they remain up to standard. Document all your checks to provide written proof of due diligence if required.

6.5. Healthy Play: Adhering to Health and Hygiene Standards

Playgrounds can be a hub for germs and the spread of infection if not appropriately cleaned and sanitized. Therefore, it's crucial to maintain high health and hygiene standards. Laws or guidelines can provide a handy framework to follow. General rules include daily cleaning, regular deep cleaning, and immediate cleanup of any spills or accidents.

In addition to these routines, you should also have necessary facilities like hand sanitizing stations or washrooms to ensure kids and their guardians can maintain good hygiene while at the playground.

6.6. Insurance: Keep Your Business and Visitors Protected

Last but far from least is securing the appropriate insurance coverage. Insurance is what shields you from unexpected catastrophes such as injuries, equipment damages, or even liability lawsuits.

Depending on your jurisdiction, the type of insurance coverage you need can vary. However, it generally includes general business insurance, liability insurance, and property insurance. Talking to an insurance agent who understands your business's unique needs can help in determining the best coverage.

To conclude, launching your indoor playground demands more than just creating an enjoyable environment - it requires navigating this complex sea of legalities and permissions. Yet these steps don't have to be an insurmountable hurdle. With patience, diligent planning, and some professional assistance, you can pave a smooth path to your playground's debut and, before you know it, be an exciting part and promoter of children's laughter and joy.

Chapter 7. A Play for All Ages: Creating Inclusive and Diverse Play Spaces

As pioneers of indoor play areas, we need to create an environment that not only entertains but also serves as a haven for children of all ages, backgrounds, and abilities. We aim to ensure that our indoor playgrounds spark joy, promote learning, and foster inclusivity.

7.1. Structuring Child-friendly Spaces

Structuring an indoor play area that caters to varying interests, ages, and abilities is paramount. Begin with safe, separate zones for different age groups: an area for infants and young toddlers, another for older toddlers and preschool-age children, and a space for school-aged children.

The infants' zone should focus on stimulating the senses. Use vibrant colors, soft toys, play mats, and baby-safe mirrors. Encourage motor skills development with age-appropriate play equipment such as ramps, small ball pits, and low steps.

The zone for older toddlers and preschoolers can incorporate more complex play structures. Small slides, soft block climbers, and various play panels can be used to stimulate imagination and foster cognitive development.

School-aged children's zones should offer activities that challenge their growing abilities. Include play equipment like rope courses, climbing walls, or even a miniature zip line. Interactive games that promote teamwork and communication are also recommended.

Remember to provide supportive equipment for children with physical challenges. Ramps, handrails, and spacious design accommodate wheelchairs, crutches, or children with mobility issues.

7.2. Incorporating Sensory Play

Sensory play is crucial for children's development. These experiences can help children to improve motor skills, boost memory, and learn problem-solving tactics.

Sensory wall panels with different textures, colors, and patterns promote visual and tactile stimulation. Sound tubes or musical instruments cater to auditory senses.

Consider installing a sensory room or quiet space. For children with sensory processing challenges, overwhelming environments can heighten anxiety. A quiet, low-lit room, with soft textures and soothing sounds, can provide an accessible retreat.

7.3. Planning for Diversity

Cultural diversity should be reflected in your playground. Play environments can encourage cross-cultural understanding and teach respect for differences.

Consider a "global village" corner with a display of traditional houses or cultural artifacts from around the world. Kids can play 'world explorer' and learn about diversity in a fun, engaging way.

Board games or puzzles showcasing various cultures, landmarks, or global issues can help children gain knowledge about the world in a playful manner.

Incorporating signages and labels in multiple languages can make children from diverse linguistic backgrounds feel welcome and represented.

7.4. Inviting Special Needs Inclusion

Creating an inclusive playground goes beyond physical accessibility. It means designing a space where children with various disabilities can play alongside typically developing children.

Interactive panels and games can be installed at various heights to include children in wheelchairs. Visually-impaired children could benefit from sensory-play elements such as Braille blocks or texture tunnels.

Provide quiet zones to cater to children with Autistic Spectrum Disorders, as they might become overwhelmed by noise or crowds. Also, use clear, simple signage and visual-prop cues to ease navigation for children with cognitive differences.

7.5. Implementing Safety Measures

While focusing on inclusivity and diversity, safety remains a top priority. Use soft surface materials while selecting flooring to minimize the risk of injuries from falls. Ensure that satisfactory hygiene standards are met, particularly in areas such as the restroom or café.

Play equipment should conform to safety standards, and have clear instructions for use. Staff should regularly inspect all play areas, and repairs should be made promptly.

Ensure well-designated, monitored exit and entry points to avoid child mishaps. Also, provide regular safety training for all staff members.

The creation of diverse, inclusive playgrounds is not an easy task. But with thoughtful planning and knowledgeable design, we can create spaces that accommodate and celebrate children from all walks of life. This commitment to inclusivity not only garners customer loyalty but also transforms lives by making play accessible and enjoyable for all children.

Chapter 8. Fun Finances: Pricing, Budgeting, and Profit Margins

A solid understanding of the financial realm is crucial when it comes to the successful launching of an indoor playground. In this section, we will traverse the essential fields of pricing strategies, budgeting, and understanding profit margins. Each of these elements plays a crucial role in the backdrop of a prosperous children's center.

8.1. Pricing for Success

Pricing decisions can be more complex than 'cost plus profit.' Determining the right price requires research, strategy, and an understanding of your market and competition.

It's important to conduct detailed competitor analysis. Visit or research other indoor play centers in your area or similar urban segments nationwide. What are their pricing structures? Do they offer membership options or discounts on special days?

Understanding the value you provide is essential. Consider what sets your playground apart. Do you offer unique attractions, longer hours, or more personalized staff? Reflect these in your costs.

Setting prices too low may increase volume, but it may also constrain your revenues, whereas prices set too high may decrease demand. Thus, it's crucial to balance affordability and profitability.

8.2. Budget with Finesse

Budgeting plays a pivotal role in your indoor playground's long-term well-being. It's the blueprint for managing your money.

The first step is to list operating expenses:

- Rent or mortgage for your playground location
- Maintenance and cleaning
- Utilities
- Salaries of staff
- Insurance and licensing
- Marketing
- Other expenses like toys, stationery, or refreshments

These are merely the starting points. It's essential to keep a buffer for unforeseen costs or emergencies.

Regular budget reviews are critical – analyze your budget monthly or quarterly with discretion and make necessary adjustments. Adaptability in budgeting is key to staying financially healthy.

8.3. Hitting Profit Margins

Profit margins are the gauge of your business's profitability. Knowing your gross and net profit margins can unveil insights about your business's overall health.

Gross profit margin is the percentage of your sales revenue left after paying the direct costs of goods/services sold. It's calculated as:

On the other hand, net profit margin is often referred to as the 'bottom line.' It indicates what portion of your sales revenue remains as profit after all operating expenses have been deducted.

Understanding these margins can guide you about where to cut costs, how to price, or when to scale up. If your margin is shrinking, it's time to investigate increased costs or decreasing pricing power.

Profit margins aren't just about numbers. A shrinking margin could indicate you're underpricing services or not operating effectively. Conversely, steadily increasing margins might signify a successful strategy or opportunity for growth.

8.4. Projected Financials

When drafting a business plan, projected financials provide insight into your playground's financial future. They include projections for profit and loss, cash flow, and a balance sheet.

These projections should take into account your business's growth plan:

- What is your growth strategy?

- What will it cost?

- How much revenue might it bring in?

Though these figures are forecasts, they should be as realistic as possible. It's a tremendous tool for investors and lenders but also helps to align your business strategy.

Unveiling the world of finance associated with indoor playgrounds may feel overwhelming. Still, with deep comprehension and diligent application of principles of pricing, budgeting and profit margins, you are well on your way to make your children's center a stellar financial success alongside being the nucleus of countless childhood memories. Remember with every slide, every swing, and every laughter echoes the sound of a well-played game in business strategy and finance!

Understanding this sector's financial terrain empowers you to create a profitable, sustainable business that brings joy to children and returns to investors. As you navigate your indoor playground journey, remember that every decision, financial or otherwise, should ultimately lead to a place of fun, creativity, and playful discovery.

Chapter 9. Empire of Joy: Marketing Strategies for Success

The heart beats at the core of every successful business is a well-planned and executed marketing strategy. This not only creates awareness but also engages with your prospective customers and convinces them to choose your indoor playground over others. Delve into this highly detailed guide that provides effective techniques to market your children's center successfully, bringing immense joy to the kids and profitability to your venture.

9.1. Understanding the Market

Before you start deploying your marketing strategies, it's crucial to understand your target market thoroughly. This means knowing the needs, preferences, and behaviors of your potential customers – parents, caregivers, kindergartens, schools, and children.

To understand your target market, conduct a thorough market analysis by observing the trends, understanding the needs of the customer, doing competitive analysis, and identifying the gaps in your local market. Broadly, it involves:

- Identification of potential demographics: Start by identifying who will be most interested in your services. This could be families with children, schools, hospitals for children's therapeutic services, charity organizations dealing with children, and other relevant parties.

- Size of the market: Estimate the number of potential customers within your area of service. This can be done by looking at the number of families with children, kindergartens, schools, and hospitals serving the area.

- Market trends: Keep an ear on the ground. Understand the current trends in the industry and tailor your services to meet these trends. For example, if fitness for children is a growing trend, consider integrating it into your services.

- Competitive analysis: Identify your competitors, understand their offerings, prices, and strategies. This can give you insights on what to offer to attract and retain your customers.

9.2. Positioning Your Indoor Playground

Every successful marketing strategy begins with positioning. This will help you identify how to differentiate your indoor fun center from the competition and how to find your niche in the market.

- Unique Selling Proposition (USP): Identify what makes your indoor playground different from the competition. Is it the activities you offer? The location? Is it your staff's professionalism? Once identified, use this unique feature in all your marketing efforts.

- Value Proposition: Communicate the value your customers will receive from your services. This could be physical fitness, cognitive development, improving social skills, or simply fun-filled memorable moments.

- Competitive Advantage: Establish what you do better than anyone else in the market and make it your competitive edge. Parents should see your indoor playground as their first choice because of this advantage.

9.3. Crafting a Brand Identity

Creating a solid brand identity brings to life your indoor playground's personality, values, and, more importantly, how you wish to be perceived by your target audience.

- Logo and Tagline: Create a visually appealing and memorable logo paired with a catchy tagline to stick in your audience's minds. This could communicate your USP or sum up what you do in a fun, catchy phrase.

- Colors and Fonts: Choose colors and fonts that will resonate with children. This means bright and vibrant colors and exciting, playful fonts to grab the children's attention.

- Website and Online Presence: Building a user-friendly, engaging, and mobile-optimized website can serve as a key source of information about your playground. Enhance this with a significant online presence on appropriate social media channels to regularly interact with your target audience.

9.4. Marketing Channels and Strategies

Identify the best channels to reach your target audience, then deploy your marketing strategies. This sector works well with both online and offline efforts.

- Digital Marketing: Leverage search engine optimization (SEO), pay-per-click (PPC) advertising, social media marketing, content marketing, and email marketing to reach a wider audience and convert them into customers.

- Traditional Marketing: Local newspapers, magazines, flyers, billboards, TV and radio commercials can still be very effective for local businesses like indoor playgrounds. Participate in local community events to improve visibility.

- Partnerships: Partner with local schools, kindergartens, hospitals, and other organizations dealing with children to reach a larger audience.

- Word of Mouth: Encourage happy customers to spread the word. This can be through online reviews or just casual mention to their peers. This form of marketing is incredibly effective and costs you virtually nothing.

9.5. Evaluation

Monthly or quarterly evaluation of your marketing strategies is vital in tweaking and bettering your marketing efforts. This involves looking at audience reach, engagement, sales, website traffic, and customer feedback.

Remember that a successful marketing strategy is an ongoing process rather than a one-time event. Be ready to adapt and change with the market, always maintaining the joy and happiness of the children as your primary focus. This will set the foundation for your empire of joy, filled with laughter, creativity, and success.

Chapter 10. Ironing Out Operational Wrinkles: Staffing and Daily Management

As the owner of an indoor playground, a large part of your role encompasses various operational tasks. Key areas of concentration include staffing and day-to-day management, both of which demand detailed and comprehensive planning. Let's delve into each of these in turn to help ensure your venture becomes a loved destination for children and parents alike, and your business enjoys a sound financial health.

10.1. Staffing Your Playground

To start, you need to analyze your staffing needs. Your primary aim should be to recruit a team that guarantees the safety, comfort, and enjoyment of your visitors. This team should consist of a mix of:

1. Attendants, responsible for monitoring the children to ensure safety and fun.

2. Customer-service personnel who handle visitor inquiries and manage bookings.

3. Maintenance crews who maintain cleanliness and hygiene, and ensure all play equipment is in top working condition.

4. Café staff (if applicable), responsible for preparing and serving food and beverages to the visitors.

Hiring right goes beyond just filling these roles, though. It's important to look for certain qualities in your potential employees.

1. **Enthusiasm for children**: Staff members should enjoy interacting with children, understanding their needs and ensuring their safety and comfort.

2. **Professionalism**: They should be well-groomed, respectful, prompt, and efficient in carrying out their tasks.

3. **Problem-solving skills**: Should a problem arise, staff members should be equipped to handle it with patience and cool-headedness.

4. **Good communication skills**: It's important for them to be able to communicate effectively with both children and their parents.

Training is a crucial part of the staffing process, you should invest time into systematically training your employees for tasks such as managing their respective stations, both with respect to children's safety and in providing impeccable service.

10.2. Daily Management: Solutions for Smooth Operations

After forging a stellar team, the next key operational feature you must consider is the day-to-day management of your indoor playground. Here are some crucial aspects about which you might want to think carefully.

Booking and walk-ins management : Develop a sound system for bookings and walk-ins. Monitor peak periods and plan your booking slots to allow maximum utilization of the facility without overcrowding.

Maintenance routines : Rigorous cleaning schedules should be established for all areas of your playground, keeping it sparkling clean and hygienic. Include regular checks of equipment for potential safety hazards as part of your maintenance routine.

Financial management : Cultivate robust financial record-keeping systems for all monetary transactions that occur. Regular tracking helps with performance analysis and forecasting trends.

Public relations : Formulate strategies to manage interactions with your playground's visitors. Nurprisingly, customer satisfaction and good reviews are pivotal to the success of your venture.

10.3. Automation as an Aid

Consider introducing an automated management system to streamline operations such as online reservations, staff scheduling, and financial bookkeeping. This allows your staff to focus more on interacting with the customers and maintaining your playground, rather than being tied up in administrative tasks.

10.4. Health and Safety: A Top Priority

It's crucial to meet all the local health and safety regulations in setting up and running your indoor playground. Regular audits and inspections to ensure compliance with these standards can help prevent incidents and penalties. It also assures parents that their children are in a safe environment.

10.5. The Add-Ons: Cafeterias and Gift Shops

If your playground comes with additional amenities such as a café or a gift shop, adequate staffing, inventory management, and daily operation procedures should be established for these as well. While these extra facilities add more complexity to your management responsibilities, they can also significantly increase your business' revenues.

To glean maximum advantage from your venture in the fun-filled industry of indoor playgrounds, detailed planning and effective operational management are critical. While it can seem a daunting task at first, your efforts in ironing out operational wrinkles will pave the way for a successful and flourishing indoor playground.

Chapter 11. The Rainbow After Rain: Overcoming Challenges and Embracing Growth

Every venture, no matter its nature or industry, is beset with challenges, but none of these hurdles are insurmountable—not when faced with creativity, resilience, and ingenuity. In establishing a children's indoor playground, the road towards a thriving enterprise may be strewn with a few stumbling blocks. It's the rainbow after the rain, the triumph over adversity that makes the journey worthwhile. In this chapter, we will explore the common challenges in starting an indoor playground and how to address them, as well as how to embrace growth through continuous improvement and scaling up plans.

11.1. Identifying and Navigating Initial Challenges

Starting a children's indoor playground requires substantial capital investment. The expense of leasing or purchasing a space compliant with safety standards, procuring gaming apparatus, and paying for regulatory licenses, maintenance, insurance, and staffing can pose a daunting obstacle. It's crucial to conduct in-depth market research to understand the financial requirements thoroughly and draft a realistic business plan. Remember, financial institutions and potential investors are more likely to finance businesses that present a comprehensive, convincing business plan that spells out profitability.

Furthermore, staying aware of the latest health and safety guidelines for children's playgrounds is paramount. Safety should never be compromised—since it directly impacts both the well-being of the children and the reputation of your business. Work closely with safety experts, follow industry best practices, and incorporate regular maintenance and safety checks to ensure continuous compliance.

Legal and regulatory hurdles may seem like stumbling blocks, but with adequate preparation and expert advice, they can be efficiently navigated. Prioritize understanding local business laws, zoning regulations, and licensing requirements early in the planning stages. Consider consulting with a business attorney or a legal advisory firm specializing in similar business models for accurate guidance.

11.2. Making Marketing and Customer Retention Work Together

No business venture can thrive without effective marketing and exceptional customer experience. However, gaining a substantial customer base and retaining it can pose quite a challenge, especially in the initial stages.

Building a solid marketing strategy is vital during the foundational phase of your business. Leverage a mix of traditional marketing methods and online marketing strategies, like social media and search engine optimization (SEO), to create awareness and drive traffic to your indoor playground. Coordinate events and parties that could lure groups. Offer promotions or create membership programs and loyalty perks to incentivize customer retention.

Remember, nothing maintains customer loyalty better than an exceptional experience — enhancing customer service should be a constant effort. Installing a feedback system wherein parents can voice their concerns, observations, or suggestions can prove immensely beneficial in improving your service.

11.3. Adapting to Changing Trends and Innovation

In response to fast-moving technological advances and changing lifestyle trends, the children's indoor playground industry is continually evolving. Keeping up with these trends and adapting your business to match them is crucial.

Emerging trends, such as the incorporation of technology like Virtual Reality (VR) and Augmented Reality (AR) into playground equipment, can present both opportunities and challenges. Keeping abreast of these developments and knowing when and how to incorporate them can help maintain your competitive edge.

Investing in staff training and development is another integral part of staying abreast of industry trends and providing top-quality service. Encouraging your staff to participate in regular training and upgrading their skills will ensure they remain competent and confident in handling new equipment and trends.

11.4. Scaling Up and Embracing Growth

Once your indoor playground is thriving and earning a reliable profit, it's time to consider scaling up. Growth can come in various forms - expanding your current location, replicating success in a new location, or diversifying your offerings to capitalize on new opportunities.

When scaling up, however, it's crucial to not compromise the quality of service or alienate your existing customer base. It's also important to consider additional operating costs, market saturation, and consistent brand delivery across different locations.

In conclusion, building a successful children's indoor playground comes with its set of challenges. However, with perseverance, creativity, and a keen sense of business acumen, these hurdles can turn into stepping stones towards growth and success. The rainbow of success follows the rain of challenges—credit goes to those who dare to dream and back their vision with action.